Frank O'Hara   The Museum of Modern Art, New York

NAKIAN

DISTRIBUTED BY DOUBLEDAY & COMPANY, INC., GARDEN CITY, NEW YORK

ACKNOWLEDGMENTS

This exhibition surveys Reuben Nakian's work of the last twenty years, commencing with sculptures of the mid-'forties after he had reexamined and drastically revised the style which had brought him to public attention more than a decade before. Since this catalogue is, however, the first extensive publication to appear on the artist, certain key works of his earlier period are illustrated in the "Biographical Outline," as well as some important works, now lost, which first won him fame (*Babe Ruth,* portrait heads of members of the Roosevelt cabinet), and other later sculptures destroyed by Nakian in the process of reworking them (the *Venus* of 1952, the more recent *Maja* of 1962-63).

Although in the past five years Nakian has been honored with major exhibitions at the VI Bienal in São Paulo, Brazil, at the Los Angeles County Museum of Art, and at the Gallery of Modern Art in Washington, the present exhibition is his first large-scale one in New York. It includes the first showing of two recently completed masterpieces, the *Birth of Venus* and the group of four monumental figures, the *Judgment of Paris.*

In organizing the exhibition we are especially indebted to the cooperation of a remarkable triumvirate: the artist himself, his chief assistant Larry McCabe, and his friend and dealer Charles Egan —the latter two for many years close collaborators with Nakian in the creation and presentation of his work. Grateful mention should also be made of Mrs. Edith Gregor Halpert and Thomas B. Hess, champions of Nakian's work at different, but equally trying, times for the artist; both have provided valuable assistance and information. The enthusiasm of Mr. and Mrs. Philip M. Stern of Washington, D.C. and of James Elliott, formerly Chief Curator of the Los Angeles County Museum of Art (now Director of the Wadsworth Atheneum, Hartford), led to the first major purchases of Nakian's work and the two large exhibitions in

their respective cities, mentioned above. We have benefited greatly by the documentation for these shows, and also from the independent research of Miss Cynthia Jaffe.

On behalf of The Museum of Modern Art, I wish to thank the following lenders whose generosity has made possible the presentation of this exhibition: Mr. David P. Bassine, New York; Mrs. Robert M. Benjamin, New York; Mrs. Eleanor Berkson, New York; Mr. and Mrs. Thor Bostrom, New York; Mr. and Mrs. Warren Brandt, New York; Mr. Charles Brickbauer, Baltimore, Maryland; Mr. Donald Droll, New York; Mr. Emile Dubrule, New York; Mr. and Mrs. Lee V. Eastman, New York; Mr. and Mrs. Robert B. Eichholz, Washington, D.C.; Estate of Mrs. Henry Epstein; Mr. and Mrs. Thomas B. Hess, New York; Mr. and Mrs. George S. Heyer, Jr., Austin, Texas; The Joseph H. Hirshhorn Collection, New York; Mr. and Mrs. J. Lee Johnson III, Fort Worth, Texas; Mr. and Mrs. Alvin S. Lane, New York; Mrs. Bliss Parkinson, New York; Mr. George S. Rosenthal, Cincinnati, Ohio; Mr. and Mrs. Philip M. Stern, Washington, D.C.; Margot Stewart, New York; The Los Angeles County Museum of Art, Los Angeles, California; Whitney Museum of American Art, New York; Egan Gallery, New York; Donald Morris Gallery, Detroit, Michigan; and one anonymous lender.

Among my colleagues at The Museum of Modern Art, I wish to thank Wilder Green for designing the installation of the exhibition, Miss Kathleen Haven for designing its invitation and poster, and Miss Elizabeth Tweedy, who assisted in all the details of organization. For assistance in preparing the catalogue, I acknowledge with particular thanks the contributions of William Berkson, who provided the first comprehensive chronology on Nakian's career, and of Miss Elita Taylor, who compiled the bibliography. I am also grateful to Miss Helen M. Franc as editor, Miss Mary Ahern as designer, and Miss Françoise Boas, who has supervised all details of the catalogue's production.

F. O'H.

CONTENTS

Photograph of Nakian by D. D. Ryan, 1965

Goddess with the Golden Thighs. 1964-65. Bronze, 12′6″ long. Egan Gallery, New York

The career of Reuben Nakian has had dramatic ups and downs, advances, reversals, revaluations. His stylistic doubling-back and pushing-forward is not only exemplified by his development, but literally prefigured in his work: the slash-cut drawing into wet clay which ends as elegant, pastoral evocation of nymph and satyr; the harshly formed and rigidly armatured metal sheets which turn into erotic waves of Tarquinian lust and Lucretian submission, or autumnal leaves drifting toward a whimsical gravitational pull. His early belief in "democratic" mythic heroes as subject matter (Babe Ruth, Franklin Delano Roosevelt and his cabinet) was followed by his discovery of the pertinence of classical myth (Europa, Mars and Venus, Hecuba, Hellenic-Trojan tragedy in general). Nakian has created a remarkable *oeuvre* since the mid-'forties through all these trials of temperament and of will; or perhaps, because of his harsh self-criticism and his insistence on continuing into the present the classical values of grandeur and nobility (in a non-academic sense), one might say more accurately that a remarkable *oeuvre* has survived to poise itself against certain contemporary values that offend him. He said in 1954: "I hate this age. We have no great people knocking at our doors and asking to come in and see what we're doing. It's very cold here. So you have to train yourself to ignore it. An artist should be alone, but he also should be with civilized people....Art comes down to taste and aristocracy. Van Gogh, he was an aristocrat of the mind, of the taste. And that's why Picasso's so great. Anyone can draw or model. But you have to have taste to know exactly where to put a line or a color." (bibl. 2)

Nakian was born in New York State, but like his friend Arshile Gorky he grew up in a combination of milieus—Armenian-familial and Brave-New-World-Dos Passos-USA social. Like most talented American artists of the period, he was at one and the same time the promising and the disadvantaged young man. Encouraged in his artistic interests by his parents, Nakian at the age of ten was studying drawing as other children study the piano, and like other talented children, he quickly developed considerable facility. The family was then living in New Jersey, but he felt the lure of New York City when he was sixteen, and his parents allowed him to follow it.

As a teen-ager in New York, Nakian took odd jobs of the sort which would now be on the periphery of the art world, but then were not so far from what the public regarded as its center. He worked as an office boy and in advertising agencies, did lettering for magazine covers, made line drawings for cigarette ads. He presumably thought of success in terms as various as James Montgomery Flagg, John Sloan, Maxfield Parrish, and Paul Manship. Thomas B. Hess gives an eloquent appraisal of the atmosphere of the art world during Nakian's teens and early twenties: "...It was a too-healthy, gamey, cosy American art-world that, in retrospect, seems terrifying and insane. Teddy Roosevelt was a culture hero, a muse for the non-alienated artist. A successful painter was a Success, a bully-boy of stag clubs who could sketch and tell jokes and hunt and be a sport, live a full strenuous life as an American—and die at the age of seventy with the understanding that his energy had been wasted on false ambitions; that his dedication had been to Others' standards and to their unreality; that whatever had been crucial for the individual had been thoughtlessly squandered in the convivial beery dream of the American Male." (bibl. 31)

Nakian did not stay with the "beery dream" very long. His interest soon centered on a stylization of

p. 38, 40

animal forms closely related to that of Gaston Lachaise, with whom he served his apprenticeship when he came to work in the studio of Paul Manship in 1916. Stylization was the order of the day, whether the archaistic stylization of a Manship, a kind of mock-heroic idealization of the proletariat, or a belated Art Nouveau stylization of human and animal forms, finding curves, swoops, and stabilized arabesques in breasts, thighs, torsos, a rabbit's ears, a bear's crouching back. The ultimate realization of this trend is found in Brancusi's *Seal* and *Fish,* in which the intensity of conception leads to an extreme abstraction of form; but the works of American sculptors of this period, excepting those of a few like Flannagan, Lachaise, and Zorach, now seem too easily formulated, too simply characterized, to command our admiration. Sculptural motion too, anecdotal and draped, was generally dependent upon stylization or was symbolized by clusters of dolphins or birds laboriously artifacted, until the slowly moving pedestals of Brancusi and the mobiles of Calder removed it from the illustrative to the actual. When sculptures were monumental, they were Neo-Classical-Realistic, or Federal-Commission style; when intimate, they often tended to look like centerpieces for a table of very indeterminate character and period.

In 1934 Nakian completed what seems from photographs (it has disappeared long since) an extra-

p. 41
ordinary and monstrous eight-foot figure of *Babe Ruth,* a definitely Zeitgeist-inspired work which was
p. 41, 42
widely publicized. He had, however, preceded this in 1932-33 by portrait heads of some of his fellow artists and of collectors, and shortly after he began to follow an inclination toward the pursuit of more serious and climactic plastic exploration of subject matter. This is already hinted at in some of the portrait heads
p. 41
of the Roosevelt cabinet, and particularly in the one of Harry L. Hopkins. In this head, within the dual constraints of the brief time permitted for modeling in the Hopkins office and of a realism verging on that of the Social Realists, Nakian had already grasped a dreamy, idealistic tone which for the first time became overt and almost Roman. It seems now that in his early years Nakian's main problem was to make the dream overt rather than vulgar, and that all his researches for almost fifteen years after the Hopkins head
p. 42
were to culminate in the great resurgence of the terra-cotta "Europas" and the large plaster *Venus* of 1952 (now destroyed), with its hewn melancholy and innocence, which led to his present major period.

About 1935 Nakian began a drastic revision, singular and willful, of his artistic concepts. He had always sought a "land of his own" in art. Just as in the early 'twenties, while sharing a studio with Lachaise, he persisted in carving animal forms when Lachaise had already begun working on monumental nudes, in the late 'thirties Nakian rejected the dominant School of Paris to cull earlier European art history for his right place. Little work of this period remains, but with the emergence of the terra-cottas toward the

p. 12, 13,
20, 22, 26
end of the 'forties we see that a great exploration had taken place. Greek mythology and its Roman interpretation assume an important role. As in a different stylistic context Gorky turned to the personal mythology of Xhorkom and Sochi, and many American painters adopted mythological titles for their emerging abstractions, Nakian's references began to range from Tanagra to Watteau, from Greek vase painting (transformed with modern energy and three-dimensional sharpness by the quick, deep incisions

of his knife in the wet surface of the clay) to Rodin and Medardo Rosso, with their elaborately articulated surfaces and suggestive use of scale. Though he had met and become friendly with many artists who would later figure importantly in American art, the early terra-cottas seem most closely related to de Kooning's paintings of women begun in the late 'thirties, with their drastic cutting strokes of delineation, their massive definition, and the half-ominous, half-humorous ambiguity of their stance.

Nakian depicts his nymphs and Europas and Ledas and Hecubas as both goddesses and wantons, at once mischievous and melancholy, voluptuous yet serenely content in their artistic medium. In drawing with a wet brush, he de-idealizes the somewhat decadently erotic giantesses of Lachaise's pencil. He *p. 23, 24* brings them closer to the fresh air of de Kooning's women and to the muscular virtuosity of what would come to be called abstract expressionism's "action," thus giving them an atmosphere of personality and whim, as real as fantasy, as illusory as believed myth (coy Leda, stately Minerva, proud Venus, mourning Hecuba, and so on). Similarly in sculpture, and contrary to the major direction of his contemporaries, Nakian employs the wet media, plaster and clay, to bring his work up to the immediacy and capriciousness *p. 13, 22,* of paint. In this development, handling becomes part of content while simultaneously commenting on it, *26-31* and virtuosity lends candor to the general lubricity of subject. Through his intense reaction to media, Nakian brings the sense of touch to Lachaise's monumentalization of eroticism, and tenderness to de Kooning's confrontation of the female. When I say that Nakian's women seem content in their medium, I mean that they are caressed and enhanced, even ennobled by it. It is amost impossible to imagine an erotic or abductive act which Nakian's women (as, very differently, those of Fuseli's drawings) cannot encounter with equanimity and, on occasion, a hint of rather lofty encouragement. As myths, they have an abstract definition and security; as fantasies, they have an appetite for their own existence.

The work of the late 'forties and early 'fifties grows larger in scale, culminating in the painted steel sheets and rods of *The Rape of Lucrece,* and it becomes apparent that eroticism is an important element *p. 17* in the success of Nakian's work in many ways. The sensuousness of his surfaces and forms, as of his themes, comes from this straightforward, exuberant, even classical eroticism, which is Mediterranean and completely involved with the world of the senses. As a motivating force, it establishes certain basic themes and attitudes, not only toward subject but also toward form, especially in the handling of surfaces and patinas and in the juxtaposition of abstract with figurative forms. For Nakian, eroticism is not only a means of insisting on the allusive content of the work, on the importance of subject in art, however abstract; but it also affirms, as in Lachaise and Gorky, the necessity of sensuality in art and, indeed, the essentially sensual nature of art. It is Nakian's eroticism, too, which has prevented such monumental works as *The Rape of Lucrece, Mars and Venus,* the *Goddess with the Golden Thighs,* and the *Judg-* *p. 17, 25, 6* *ment of Paris* from straying into pomposity or vacuousness, and which has helped to maintain his char- *p. 36-37* acteristic buoyancy and spontaneity through the difficult realization of these huge works.

La Chambre à Coucher de l'Empereur. 1954. Bronze, 70″ long. Collection Mr. and Mrs. Philip M. Stern, Washington, D.C.

Nakian's work methods are a combination of Renaissance studio practice and the immediacy of Oriental calligraphers. In drawing, whether with brush or paper or with knife in wet clay or plaster, he demands completion by his action at the time of inspiration. A similar spontaneity is his goal in sculpture. The number of works destroyed because they didn't "work out," including several large sculptures, is staggering. This is not to say that the large pieces are not adjusted and worked upon, but that frequently Nakian goes too far in alteration and ruins them. To make possible this spontaneity, Nakian has had as permanent assistant the young sculptor Larry McCabe, who was his student at the Newark School of Fine and Industrial Arts in 1949. Since those days of solving the complicated problems of firing his early terra-cottas, McCabe has provided Nakian with the knowledge and help necessary to create a working situation in which wet clay or plaster is ready for the knife at the right moment, in which the technical problems of the internal-external structure of *The Rape of Lucrece* and the assembled monoliths of the *p. 17* *Goddess with the Golden Thighs* do not inhibit realization of the concept, and in which casting in bronze *p. 6* the subtly detailed and nuanced surfaces of a Hecuba takes on proper perspective to the major effort of *p. 34* creating the work itself, rather than becoming an impediment.

Having moved from Greenwich Village to Stamford, Connecticut, in 1948 Nakian set up a kiln and studio as best he could with his meager financial resources. Shortly after, in 1949, he began to exhibit terra-cottas at the Egan Gallery and has continued to show there. Nakian contributed an odd and stimulating note to a stable of artists which has included such names as Willem de Kooning, Franz Kline, Giorgio Cavallon, Philip Guston, Jack Tworkov, Robert Rauschenberg, and others. Frequently, during exhibitions of other artists, an early Europa or Venus, and later the large *La Chambre à Coucher de l'Empereur,* could be seen through the office door posing like a dignified mascot. This latter work, done in white plaster in 1954 and cast in 1958, was Nakian's first major work of the new period; its baroque lavishness of form and texture persists in the later *Olympia* and relates closely to the recent *Birth of Venus.* *p. 33, 35*

Seven years before *La Chambre à Coucher de l'Empereur,* Nakian had completed a head of a woman, *Ecstasy.* It is a curious and, to me, rather unsatisfying work, harking back to the Art Nouveau style of *p. 12* illustrational erotic themes. This fulsome manner is capable of subtly cynical and ironic comment, but it does not at all benefit Nakian's blunt and innocent approach to the subject. Unlike the earlier *Head of* *p. 12* *Duchamp,* which for all its richness of handling has a strict attitude toward form, *Ecstasy* is notable for driving the formal implications of an emotion beyond the plastic boundaries justified by its meaning. It is a signal work in Nakian's *oeuvre,* in that it is the last overstatement within his mature period and reminds us of how excessive he could have become in terms of technique and modulation had not the ultimate seriousness of his intent become clear to him. An undeniable feat of virtuosity, the *Ecstasy* lacks the unity of impulse present in even the most physically dispersed of his later works, and its descent into decorativeness is the first sign of Nakian's awareness that the technical virtuosity he sought might be a trap. In contrast to the *Ecstasy's* reminiscence of Art Nouveau draperies (hair) and symbolized passion

above left: *Head of Marcel Duchamp.* 1943. Bronze, 21¾″ high. The Joseph H. Hirshhorn Collection, New York

above right: *Ecstasy.* 1946-47. Bronze, 12½″ high. The Joseph H. Hirshhorn Collection, New York

right: *Salome.* 1948. Terra-cotta with gold leaf, 6″ high. Collection Mr. and Mrs. Philip M. Stern, Washington, D.C.

opposite left: *Europa and the Bull.* 1950. Terra-cotta, painted, 9½″ high. Egan Gallery, New York

opposite right: center, *Voyage to Crete.* 1952. Terra-cotta, 28″ high. Collection Margot Stewart, New York; right, *Europa and the Bull.* 1949-50. Terra-cotta, 27″ high. The Joseph H. Hirshhorn Collection, New York. (Photographed at Egan Gallery exhibition, 1952)

(smile), in the *Head of Duchamp* Nakian takes sculptural mass by thumb, finger, and forearm to extract from it a texture and space that lead directly toward the deeper content, the expanded open forms, and the dramatized surfaces of the important later works.

Nakian is unrepressed, un-neurotic, unabashed in his approach to sensuality, however tortuous his esthetic commitment, and whether his subject be death, bestiality, or Arcadian dalliance. This explicitness gives the "Nymph and Satyr" plaques a marvelous joy and ease, the "Europa" terra-cottas a voluptuous *p. 20, 22* dignity, and the "Leda and the Swan" drawings an almost comic abandon. Unlike most sexually oriented images in modern art, from Rodin to Andy Warhol, one finds no guilt or masochism in a Nakian. It is outgoing and athletic even in its releases and defeats: the satyr, the bull, the swan, the goat are each circumvented or absorbed by the goddess of his choice in the most choice of circumstances, that of his own choosing, like the amorous "dying" of the Elizabethans or the metamorphoses of Ovid. Where tragedy is implied, as in *The Trojan Woman, Hecuba,* and *Hiroshima,* it is the tragedy of physical, not meta- *p. 32, 34, 46* physical, death: though metaphoric, the texture of the forms by insisting on physical dissolution keeps them from being intellectually distant or emotionally remote, no matter the degree of abstraction demanded by the subject or the obscurity of its expression. As Marianne Moore once remarked in a famous riposte, a poet should not be more clear than his natural reticence permits.

DUCHESS OF ALBA SERIES. 1959-60

above left: Drawing. Ink wash on paper, 8½ x 11".–above
right: Drawing. Ink wash on paper, 8½ x 11".–below left:
Drawing. Ink wash on paper, 12¼ x 14¼".–below right:
Plaque. Terra-cotta, 14¼" long.
Los Angeles County Museum of Art, Los Angeles, California
(Museum Associates Purchase; Contemporary Art Council
Fund)

The Duchess of Alba. 1959. Welded steel, 10′ long. Los Angeles County Museum of Art, Los Angeles, California

Nakian's literalness in thematic reference has led to remarkable abstract innovation. The huge curved black sheets which form the figures of Tarquin and Lucrece and delineate them with the freshness of a wash drawing are both supported and imprisoned by the rods. No longer merely armature, these rods are as intrinsic to *The Rape of Lucrece* as are the chamber, the bedposts, and the drapes in Shakespeare's poem. This liberation of armature and its new expressive role give *The Duchess of Alba* her chaise longue and *Mars and Venus* their fateful, spindling couch. Considered abstractly as forms, the black rods thrust away from gravity, lifting the black "leaves" aloft, and reenforce our sense of the masterful drawing, vertical supporting arabesque, contained in these works.

p. 15
p. 25

These three painted steel sculptures represent an original amalgamation of baroque indulgence with constructivist severity. Though the drawings and studies for them fit into the canon of Nakian's work with considerable stylistic unity, the three sculptures are a whole period in themselves—and the only one in which his later work relates at all clearly to other major American contemporaries, Calder on the one hand and David Smith on the other. Nakian's cut and bent black sheets remind one, however elliptically, of Calder's stabiles and of the motion of some of his heavy and stately mobiles; while Nakian's rods and interstices, like a supportive superstructure, recall the stainless steel "lines" with which, in several works of the late 'fifties, Smith connected and lifted aloft his brilliant flat planes. (In fact the word "soaring," used by Smith in one of his titles, could refer to several works of each of these artists, though they could hardly be related more closely than that.) Nakian later used the idea of curved metal sheets more literally in his sculpture for the Loeb Student Center at New York University, where the abstract aluminum leaves drift across the brick façade on the south side of Washington Square Park, on the site of one of his old studios.

p. 14, 24

p. 45

Like many of the abstract expressionist painters, Nakian has always worked in series of motifs, and projected themes continue over long periods of time. The "Europa" series, begun in 1948, leads directly toward a more abstract development of this theme in the large bronze *Voyage to Crete* of 1960-62, now in the New York State Theatre at Lincoln Center. A small *Paris* of the 'forties already prefigures the intent of the monumental group, the *Judgment of Paris* of 1963-66, a project which has fascinated Nakian with obsessive regularity: the 1952 plaster *Venus,* a most remarkable work "in residence" for several seasons at the Egan Gallery, was later destroyed in Nakian's attempt to fuse the three goddesses and their judge into one large sculpture. With characteristic stubbornness he pursued this elusive theme into the 'sixties and created a group of four huge free-standing abstract figures (Paris, Venus, Juno, Minerva) poised in a fatalistic yet bawdy ritual, waiting for the apple of discord to be awarded and the Trojan War to start. The group is one of his masterpieces.

p. 46

p. 36-37
p. 42

Not all the projects, even though diligently pursued, come to such complete realization. An exacting critic of his own work, though a generous one of others', Nakian is plagued by ambition and dissatisfaction.

The Rape of Lucrece. 1955-58. Welded steel, 12′ 11″ long. The Museum of Modern Art, New York (extended loan from Egan Gallery, New York)

right: *Herodias*. 1952. Bronze, 44″ high. Estate of Mrs. Henry Epstein (courtesy Egan Gallery, New York)

below: *Voyage to Crete*. 1960. Bronze, 41″ high. Collection Mr. and Mrs. Philip M. Stern, Washington, D.C.

below right: *Voyage to Crete*. 1960. Bronze, 33″ high. Egan Gallery, New York

opposite: *The Burning Walls of Troy*. 1957. Terra-cotta, 11½″ long. Egan Gallery, New York

A superb recent *Maja,* like the earlier *Venus,* was destroyed in the attempt to make it even more beautiful. *p. 46*
An earlier large sculpture, *Hecuba on the Burning Walls of Troy* (1954), a germinal work that foretold *p. 44*
most of the technical innovations to follow, was destroyed and survives now in spirit in the single-figure
Hecuba of 1960-62—itself begun as a Hiroshima, which in the working out of the theme turned into a *p. 34*
Hecuba. The "Hiroshima" theme has been attempted several times and either changed into another
sculpture or destroyed; and Nakian still has pressing upon his consciousness projects for an *Homage to
Arshile Gorky,* a *Death of Caesar,* a *Saint John* (with Herodias and Salome), as well as a longing to make
fountains. This remarkable artist, now in his late sixties, has the energy of a young man and a confidence
more sure for having been hard won, more certain for having included defeat, rejection, and triumph.

And the last word is the key one. Having withdrawn the *Birth of Venus* for further study and rework- *p. 35*
ing after its initial showing in New York, Nakian has this year through his alterations produced a far
greater sculpture than envisioned in his original conception, grand though that was. And in the recently
completed *Hiroshima,* he has created a tragic and taciturn plastic expression capable of dealing in a work *p. 46*
of art with our guilt over this horrifying event. The expectable Hellenic catharsis, the one Hellenic idea
that Nakian seems never to have espoused with any degree of enthusiasm, disappears in the morbid
beauty of the work's realization; while the erotic works remain libidinous and arousing for all their
esthetic grace. The sculptural message of the late, mythologically inspired works, particularly *The Trojan* *p. 32*
Woman and *Hecuba,* has been that all flesh is as grass, vulnerable, destructible; and *Hiroshima* brings this *p. 34*
out very forcefully. It is philistine to decry as childish the content of pop and junk art, as Nakian is apt
to do in conversation, unless you, like Nakian, have achieved a relationship with physical truth that is
both stoic and sybaritic, wherein the dead live and the living wait in a kind of despairing sensual delight.

Frank O'Hara

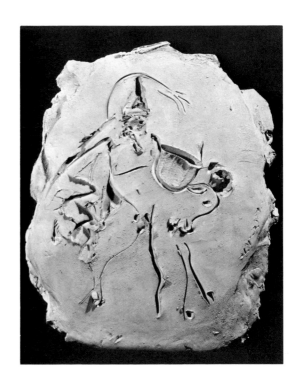

opposite: above left, *Paris*. 1950. Bronze, 9¼″ high. Private collection, New York.–bottom left, *Europa and the Bull*. 1945. Bronze, 10½″ high. Private collection, New York.— above right, *Pastorale*. 1948. Terra-cotta, 15⅝″ high. Collection Donald Droll, New York.–below right, *Europa Series*. 1948. Terra-cotta, 12¾″ high. Egan Gallery, New York

above left: *Leda and the Swan*. Terra-cotta, 14¼″ long. Collection Mr. and Mrs. Thomas B. Hess, New York

left: *Nymph and Centaur*. 1960. Terra-cotta, 15″ long. Egan Gallery, New York

opposite: Four drawings for the *Europa Series*.
1959-60. Ink on paper. Egan Gallery, New York.
above left, 14⅛ x 16¾″; above right, 14 x 16⅝″;
below left, 14 x 16⅝″; below right, 14⅛ x 16⅝″

EUROPA SERIES

below left: Plaque. 1959-60. Terra-cotta, 12½″ long. Egan Gallery, New York

below right: Plaque. 1949. Terra-cotta, 15″ high. Collection Mr. and Mrs. Thor Bostrom, New York

above left: *Hecuba Series*. 1960-62. Wash, brush and ink, 16⅝ x 14″. The Museum of Modern Art, New York (extended loan from Egan Gallery, New York)

left: *Europa Series*. 1959-60. Brush and ink, 14 x 16¾″. The Museum of Modern Art, New York (extended loan from Egan Gallery, New York)

MARS AND VENUS SERIES. 1959-60

above: *Mars and Venus Series*. 1959-60. Wash, brush and ink, 14 x 16⅞″. The Museum of Modern Art, New York (gift of Charles Egan in memory of J. B. Neumann)

opposite: above left, *Mars and Venus Series*. 1959-60. Wash, brush and ink, 11¾ x 17⅜″. Egan Gallery, New York.—above right, *Mars and Venus Series*. 1959-60. Terra-cotta, 15″ long. Egan Gallery, New York

opposite below: *Mars and Venus*. 1959-60. Welded steel, 13′ long. Egan Gallery, New York

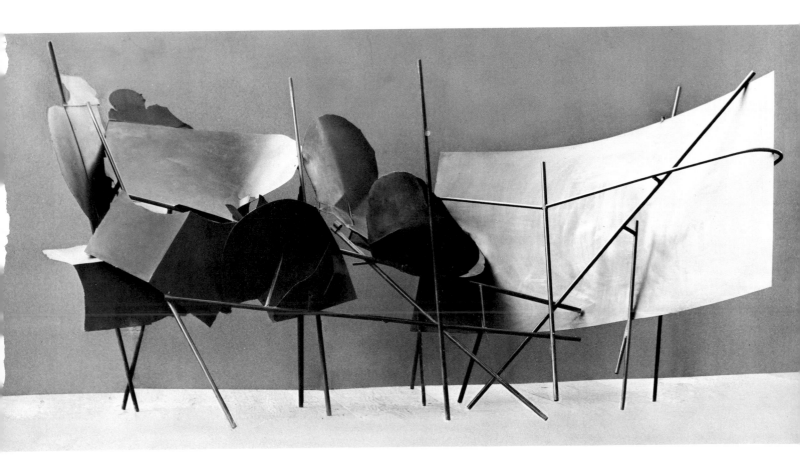

above: *Study for Voyage to Crete.* 1952. Terra-cotta, 8″ high. Collection Mr. and Mrs. Thomas B. Hess, New York

above right: *Heraldic Figures.* c. 1950-54. Terra-cotta, 8¼″ high. Collection Mr. and Mrs. Thomas B. Hess, New York

right: *Voyage to Crete.* 1949. Terra-cotta, 26″ long. Collection Mr. and Mrs. Thomas B. Hess, New York

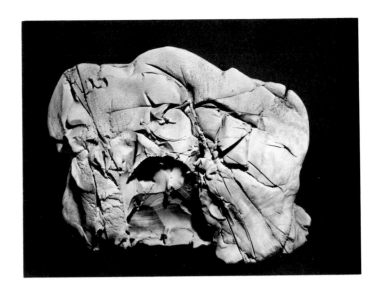

above: *Rock Drawing*. 1958. Terra-cotta, 16″ long. The Museum of Modern Art, New York (fund given in memory of Philip L. Goodwin)

left: *Rape of Lucrece Series*. 1958. Terra-cotta, 16″ long. The Museum of Modern Art, New York (gift of the artist in memory of Holger Cahill)

LEDA AND THE SWAN

above left, *Leda and the Swan*. 1963. Bronze, 12½″ long. Egan Gallery, New York.– above, *Leda and the Swan*. 1963. Bronze, 9½″ long. Collection Mrs. Eleanor Berkson, New York.–left, *Leda and the Swan*. 1962. Terra-cotta, 12″ long. Egan Gallery, New York

left: *Europa and the Bull.* 1958-60. Terra-cotta, 17″ long. Collection Mrs. Robert M. Benjamin, New York

below: *Europa Series.* 1960. Terra-cotta, 8″ high. Egan Gallery, New York

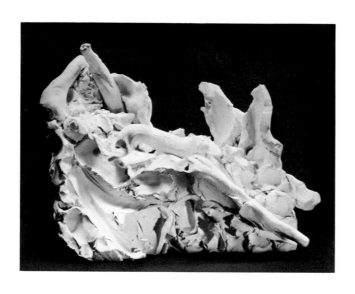

above: *Leda and the Swan Series*. 1963. Terra-cotta, 15½″ long (destroyed in casting)

above right: *Leda and the Swan*. 1960. Bronze, 6½″ high. Collection Mr. and Mrs. Warren Brandt, New York

right: *Europa Series*. 1962. Bronze, 11″ high. Collection Mr. and Mrs. J. Lee Johnson III, Fort Worth, Texas

left: *Europa Series*. 1960-62. Terra-cotta, 11″ long. Egan Gallery, New York

below: *Salome and Herodias with the Head of John the Baptist*. 1960. Terra-cotta, left to right: 10″ long; 4″ high; 9¼″ long. Collection Mr. and Mrs. Thomas B. Hess, New York

The Trojan Woman. 1960-62. Plaster and steel, 9′ 1″ high. Egan Gallery, New York

Olympia. 1960-62. Bronze, 6' high. Whitney Museum of American Art, New York
(gift of the Friends of the Whitney Museum)

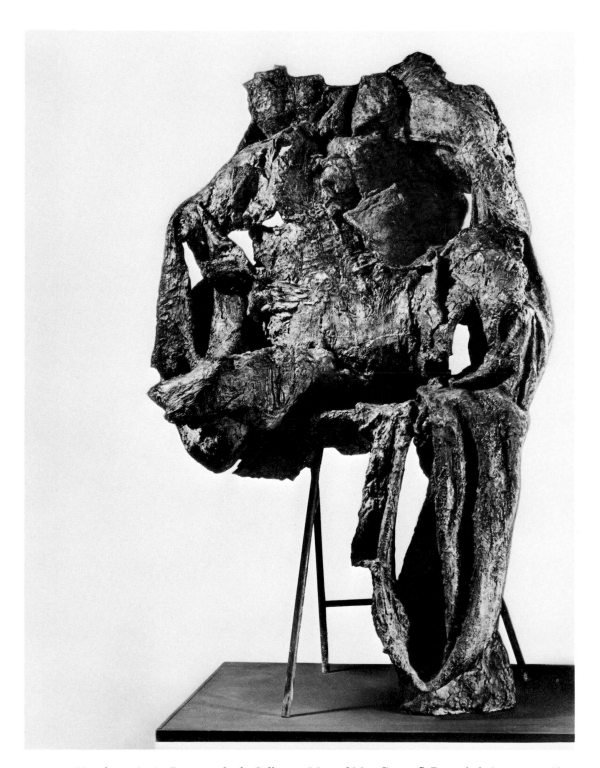

Hecuba. 1960-62. Bronze, 7' high. Collection Mr. and Mrs. George S. Rosenthal, Cincinnati, Ohio

Birth of Venus. 1963-66. Plaster, 10′ 11″ long. Egan Gallery, New York

36

JUDGMENT OF PARIS. 1963-66

opposite: *Paris*. 1963-64. Plaster, 6′6½″ high. Egan Gallery, New York

above left: *Juno*. 1964-65. Plaster, 6′11″ high. Egan Gallery, New York

left: *Venus*. 1964-65. Plaster, 7′4″ long. Egan Gallery, New York

above: *Minerva*. 1965-66. Plaster, 8′1″ high. Egan Gallery, New York

Party at the Independent Art School, New York,
1915, with Nakian in Indian costume seated in
bottom row, far right

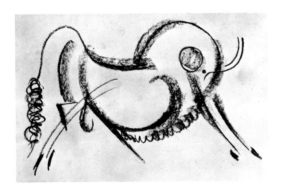

Animal Study 2. 1921. Crayon on paper, 10 x 15".
Whitney Museum of American Art, New York

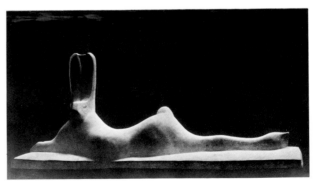

Jack Rabbit. 1921. Limestone, 36" long

BIOGRAPHICAL OUTLINE
by William Berkson

1897 Nakian born August 10 in College Point, Long Island, New York, last of five children of George and Mary (née Malakian) Nakian, Armenians who had emigrated from Turkey to the United States c. 1880. (George Nakian had come from Zeytin, a mountain village, and Mary Malakian from a small village near Bergama, the ancient Pergamos. First met casually during sixty-six day voyage on sailing steamer to New York; some time later, met again in Boston and became engaged. After marriage, settled in College Point.)

1906- Family moves to 116th Street and Lenox Avenue,
1911 New York City, thence to several New Jersey suburbs: Rutherford (1908); Union City (1910); Weehawken and Weehawken Heights (1911). At thirteen, Nakian studies drawing once a week with German teacher at academy in Jersey City; learns to copy 18th- and 19th-century German engravings. Studies plaster casts of sculpture of many periods then on view in basement of Metropolitan Museum of Art. Begins "daubing in clay."

1912 After graduating from grammar school, attends Art Students League for one month.

1913 Works in office of advertising agency for Philip Morris. Studies lettering at home and then works for mail-order houses, designing lettering for catalogues. Employed (until 1915) by *Century* magazine; runs errands for editor, poster-artist Will Bradley ("a real Yankee type"), and does lettering for magazine's covers. Impressed by reproductions of avant-garde art in German periodicals (*Jugend, Simplicissimus*) received in office and by reproductions of Watteau and Fragonard, which Bradley shows him. Through Bradley, meets James Montgomery Flagg, John Sloan, George Bellows, and Everett Shinn (who one day gives Nakian a drawing lesson and shows him how to make "rings around forms" and how "red prints black").

1915 Attends evening life-drawing classes at Independent Art School, "the only studio in New York that permitted modern training"; studies there under Homer Boss and A. S. Baylinson; draws from the model numerous monumental nudes in red French chalk, influenced by Rubens and Greek sculpture. Studies clay sculpture for a few months at Beaux Arts Academy.

1916 Makes rounds of artists' studios, hoping to be accepted as apprentice. The sculptor James Earl Fraser (whose studio on 8th Street later becomes The Jumble Shop, an important meeting place for artists) suggests Nakian visit Paul Manship. Brings his drawings to Manship (twelve years his senior), who takes him on as studio apprentice (March). Trained by Manship and his chief assistant, the French-born sculptor Gaston Lachaise (1882-1935), in techniques of patination, cutting, and casting. Begins series of drawings and sculptures of animals. Influenced by Cézanne and Brancusi.

1917 First sculpture: plaster statue-bank of cow for "Free Milk for France" campaign, widely reproduced in replica.

1919 Through Manship, spends summer at Tiffany Foundation Farm, Oyster Bay, Long Island; meets Louis Comfort Tiffany there, and does studies of cows and bulls.

1920 Manship leaves for Europe; Nakian shares (until 1923) new studio with Lachaise on Sixth Avenue between 10th and 11th Streets.

1921 *Pouter Pigeon; Jack Rabbit* (reproduced in *The Dial,* May, 1922).

1922 Included in Salons of America exhibition, Anderson Galleries, New York (October-November). Juliana Force (organizer with Gertrude Vanderbilt Whitney of the Whitney Studio Club) visits Lachaise-Nakian studio with critic Forbes Watson. On her advice, Nakian is granted monthly stipend of $250 plus studio rental. Takes studio in Weehawken Heights, New Jersey.

1923 Six sculptures exhibited at Whitney Studio Club with John Dos Passos' watercolors and Adelaide J. Lawson's paintings (January). Included in Salons of America exhibition at galleries of American Art Association, New York (May-June). Meets the sculptor William Zorach, with whom he establishes close friendship.

1924 *Bull and Cow.* Included in 37th Annual Exhibition of American Paintings and Sculpture, Art Institute of Chicago (October-December).

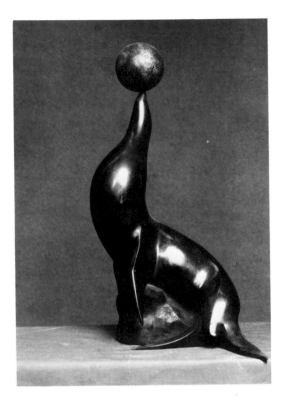

top: *Seal.* 1930. Bronze, 17¼" high. Whitney Museum of American Art, New York

above: *Young Calf.* 1929. Pink marble, 15" high. The Museum of Modern Art, New York

1925 Moves to studio on corner of Christopher and Gay Streets, New York City.

1926 *Pouter Pigeon* included in "Exhibition of Tri-National Art" at Wildenstein Galleries, New York, organized by English critic Roger Fry (January-February). First one-man show, Whitney Studio Club (November). Meets Brancusi and helps install his first one-man exhibition in the United States, a retrospective at the Brummer Gallery, New York (November). (During next few years, Nakian does occasional odd jobs for Joseph Brummer, making bases for sculpture, etc.)

1927 Becomes associated with Downtown Gallery, New York, owned by Edith Halpert.

1928 When Whitney Studio Club is supplanted by Whitney Studio Galleries, Nakian's stipend is suspended. Moves to studio on Christopher Street and Seventh Avenue.

1929 *Young Calf.* Meets the sculptor Raoul Hague, with whom he later establishes a close friendship. Included in 42nd Exhibition of American Paintings and Sculpture, Art Institute of Chicago (October-December).

1930 Included in "46 Painters and Sculptors under 35 Years of Age," Museum of Modern Art, New York (April). Sculpts series of *Seals,* exhibited, along with animal drawings, in one-man show, Downtown Gallery (October-November). Included in "33 Moderns" exhibition at Grand Central Galleries, New York (January-February), organized by Edith Halpert.

1931 Exhibits at Downtown Gallery with William Zorach and Hunt Diedrich. *Seal* purchased by Whitney Museum of American Art. Receives Guggenheim Fellowship for travel abroad; spends eight months in Europe, traveling in France and Italy.

1932 Moves to studio at 42 Washington Square South. Begins series of portrait busts of artists; *"Pop" Hart* (George Overbury Hart) exhibited in group show at Downtown Gallery. Two sculptures included in "Exhibition of American Society of Painters, Sculptors & Gravers," Whitney Museum of American Art. Meets Rose St. John, whom he later marries, in Greenwich Village.

1933 Helps Brancusi install his one-man show, Wildenstein Galleries, New York. Meets Arshile Gorky with Stuart Davis. Museum of Modern Art acquires *"Pop" Hart.* One-man show, "Portraits of Ten Artists" (actually nine—Alexander Brook, Elmer Rice, "Pop" Hart, Gaston Longchamp, Peggy Bacon, William Harlan Hale, Raphael Soyer, Concetta Scaravaglione, Joseph Pollet), Downtown Gallery (February-March). Through Edith Halpert, commissioned by Robert Straus (of the department-store family, then an official of National Recovery Administration) to do portrait of General Hugh ("Ironpants") Johnson, head of the NRA. Invades offices of members of President Franklin Delano Roosevelt's cabinet and sculpts portraits of Edward McGrady, Harold Ickes, Cordell Hull, Henry Wallace, Rexford G. Tugwell, Donald Richberg, and Harry L. Hopkins. Works on busts in studio in Department of Commerce Building, Washington, D.C. Makes portrait head of President

top: Portrait heads of President Roosevelt and his cabinet; left to right, *Henry Wallace, Franklin Delano Roosevelt, Harold Ickes, Harry L. Hopkins.* 1933. Plaster, life size

above: *"Pop" Hart.* 1932. Plaster, 17″ high. The Museum of Modern Art, New York (gift of Abby Aldrich Rockefeller)

left: Nakian with eight-foot-high plaster of *Babe Ruth,* 1934

Nakian's drawing room, 1960, with drawings and sculpture of the late 1940s and early '50s, photographs of the Villa d'Este, and reproduction of Ingres' *Grande Odalisque*. The sculpture at the left is *Europa and the Bull,* 1945 (plaster, for bronze ill. p. 20); that in the center is *Salome,* 1948 (ill. p. 12)

Larry McCabe, Nakian's chief assistant, with *Hiroshima* in progress, 1965

top: *Dikran Kelekian.* 1943. Plaster, 13″ high. Egan Gallery, New York

above: *Venus.* 1952. Plaster, 60″ high. (Destroyed)

Roosevelt from photographs. Included in First Biennial Exhibition of Contemporary American Sculpture, Watercolors and Prints, Whitney Museum of American Art (December-January 1934).

1934 Completes eight-foot sculpture of *Babe Ruth* (George Herman Ruth), exhibited at Downtown Gallery (February-March), then at First Municipal Art Exhibition, Rockefeller Center (ill. p. 41). First feature article: "Nakian: A Master of Form" by Nathaniel Pousette-Dart, *Studio News* (February). Mentioned in *Art in America in Modern Times,* by Alfred H. Barr, Jr., and Holger Cahill. Marries Rose St. John (December).

1935 Establishes close friendship with Arshile Gorky. One-man exhibition of "Portrait Heads of Officials of the Present Administration," Corcoran Gallery of Art, Washington, D.C. (April), with catalogue introduction by Henry McBride; shown following month, Downtown Gallery, New York. Moves to studio on 58th Street, New York. Conversations with Gorky introduce him to new ideas about Cézanne, Picasso, Ingres, and Surrealism and lead Nakian to reappraise his manner of working. Throughout the 'thirties and most of the 'forties does little sculpture but draws constantly, revising ideas of both technique and subject matter. Except for group shows, ceases to exhibit until 1949.

1936 Moves to Grasmere, Staten Island, New York. Assigned to Federal Art Project of Works Progress Administration. Three sculptures included in "The Art of Today," Albright Art Gallery, Buffalo (January) and one in second Whitney Biennial (January-February). *Young Calf* purchased by Museum of Modern Art (October). Commissioned by his friend, the antique-dealer Dikran Kelekian, to sculpt portrait bust of the painter Louis Eilshemius.

1937 Through Gorky, meets Willem de Kooning. Son, Paul, born June 6.

1938 Included in "Trois Siècles d'Art aux Etats Unis," Musée du Jeu de Paume, Paris (organized by Museum of Modern Art, New York). Begins modeling abstract *Europa and Bull* (completed 1942, later destroyed). Included in "Modern American and European Sculpture," Museum of Modern Art Gallery, Washington (December-January 1939).

1939 Through dealer J. B. Neumann meets Charles Egan, with whom he establishes close friendship. *Seal* acquired by Museum of Modern Art.

1940 Second son, George, born June 3.

1943 Plaster portraits: *Head of Marcel Duchamp* (later cast in bronze) and *Dikran Kelekian.*

1944 *Hermes.* Takes house at Stamford, Conn., and studio at 61 Washington Square South. *Dikran Kelekian* included in exhibition "Kelekian as the Artist Sees Him," Durand-Ruel Galleries, New York (October-November).

1945 Charles Egan opens Egan Gallery and becomes Nakian's dealer.

1946 Teaches (until 1951) at Newark School of Fine and Industrial Arts. Becomes friendly with painter Ludwig Sander. Using girl student at School as model, begins *Ecstasy* (completed in plaster in 1947 and later cast in bronze).

1947 Finding kiln at his disposal at School, begins series of terra-cottas (and countless drawings) based on mythological themes.

1948 Begins "Europa" series of terra-cottas, which he continues into mid-'sixties. Leaves New York studio; sets up kiln a few miles away from house in Stamford.

1949 Meets, among students who assist him in firing terra-cottas, Larry McCabe, who later becomes Nakian's permanent assistant. Terra-cotta drawings (called "stone drawings" because of hardness of material resulting from firing process) exhibited at Egan Gallery, New York (May)—Nakian's first one-man show since 1935. Included in Annual Exhibition of Contemporary American Sculpture, Watercolors and Drawings, Whitney Museum of American Art (April-May).

1950 One-man show, Egan Gallery.

1952 Large terra-cotta, *Voyage to Crete;* plaster sculptures, *Venus* (now destroyed) and *Herodias.* One-man show, Egan Gallery. Teaches (until 1954) once a week at Pratt Institute, Brooklyn.

1954 One-man show of sculpture and drawings, Egan Gallery. *La Chambre à Coucher de l'Empereur* (plaster; cast 1958), *Hecuba on the Burning Walls of Troy* (destroyed later that year; ill. p. 44).

1955 One-man show, Egan Gallery (which *Art News* later votes among year's ten best). Begins working with steel plate on large *Rape of Lucrece,* completed three years later.

1958 *Rape of Lucrece, La Chambre à Coucher de l'Em-*

Back and front views of *Hecuba on the Burning Walls of Troy.* 1954. Steel, plaster, glue, wire mesh, 11′ high. (Destroyed)

pereur, and *Voyage to Crete* exhibited at Stewart-Marean Gallery, New York, under Charles Egan's supervision (November-December). Receives grant of $10,000 from Ford Foundation.

1959   One-man show, Egan Gallery. *Rape of Lucrece* and related studies obtained by Museum of Modern Art as extended loans from Egan Gallery. *Duchess of Alba.* Begins large steel *Mars and Venus,* completed following year.

1960   Wins New York University competition among five invited American sculptors (the others being Herbert Ferber, Dimitri Hadzi, James Rosati, and Bernard Rosenthal) for architectural decoration of façade of the Loeb Student Center, Washington Square South, on site of Nakian's second studio. (Group of shaped steel and aluminum forms, 28 by 45 feet, installed on façade during Spring 1961 and dedicated July.) One of "4 Sculptors" in exhibition, Great Jones Gallery, New York. One-man show, Egan Gallery (November). First version of four large plasters, *Hecuba, Olympia, The Trojan Woman,* and *Voyage to Crete* (all completed 1962).

1961   Completes large bronze *Europa.* One-man show in U.S. Representation (organized by Museum of Modern Art, New York) at VI Bienal, São Paulo, Brazil (September-December); travels to São Paulo with McCabe and Egan to assist with installation.

1962   One-man show, Egan Gallery (March-April). Exhibition from São Paulo (with six works added) shown at Los Angeles County Museum of Art, which purchases *Duchess of Alba* (May-June). Included in "Continuity and Change," Wadsworth Atheneum, Hartford (April-May). Eight works included in "Modern Sculpture from the Joseph H. Hirshhorn Collection," Solomon R. Guggenheim Museum, New York. Begins large plaster *Maja* and series of terra-cottas involving themes of nymphs and satyrs and of "Leda and the Swan." Takes new studio in office building, 30 Park Row, in center of Stamford.

1963   *Maja* completed (destroyed 1965; ill. p. 46). Retrospective of thirteen sculptures, plus terra-cottas and drawings, Washington (D.C.) Gallery of Modern Art (January-February). Included in "Sculpture: Open-Air Exhibition of Contemporary British and American Works," Battersea Park, London (U.S.

above: Detail of façade of Loeb Student Center, New York University, showing Nakian's aluminum forms, 1961

left: Nakian working on *The Duchess of Alba,* 1959

Partial view of U.S. Representation, VI Bienal, São Paulo, 1961; left, *The Rape of Lucrece;* left center, *Head of Marcel Duchamp;* right, drawings and terra-cottas. (Center, paintings by Burgoyne Diller)

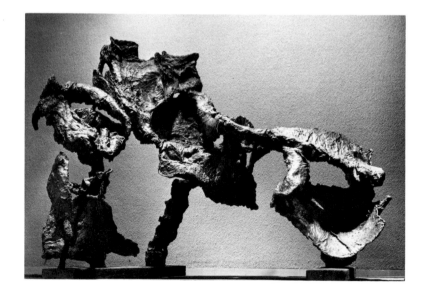

above left: *Maja.* 1962-63. Plaster, 7′ 8″ high. (Destroyed 1965)

left: *Voyage to Crete.* 1960-62. Bronze (cast 1963), 8′ long. New York State Theater, Lincoln Center, New York

above: *Hiroshima* in progress, 1966

opposite: Nakian's studio, 1965; on shelf above, studies for the *Judgment of Paris*; on wall, drawings by Nakian, photographs, and reproductions of various works of art, including Parthenon sculptures, Giovanni da Bologna's *Charity,* and paintings by Rubens, Titian, and Cézanne

selection by Museum of Modern Art, New York) and in "Sculptors of Our Time," Washington Gallery of Modern Art. Whitney Museum of American Art purchases bronze *Olympia*. Begins studies for sculpture group, *Judgment of Paris*.

1964 *Birth of Venus* completed (first version). Included in "American Drawings," Solomon R. Guggenheim Museum. *Mars and Venus* exhibited in Federal Pavilion, New York World's Fair. Bronze *Voyage to Crete* purchased for New York State Theater, Lincoln Center. One-man show, Egan Gallery (November).

1965 Included in "Critics' Choice: Art Since World War II" exhibition, Providence, (R.I.) Art Club (March-April). One-man show of terra-cottas, Egan Gallery (Spring). Five sculptures included in "Etats-Unis: Sculptures du XXe Siècle" (organized by Museum of Modern Art, New York), Musée Rodin, Paris (June-October); two subsequent showings in West Germany (see bibl. 104). Also included in "Actitudes Plásticas," University of Mexico, Mexico, D.F. (June-July). At invitation of President Lyndon B. Johnson, attends White House Festival of the Arts (June 14); *La Chambre à Coucher de l'Empereur* included in exhibition of American sculpture installed on White House grounds. Two bronzes and several drawings included in loans to U.S. Embassy, Mexico under "Art in Embassy" project of International Council of Museum of Modern Art (June-July 1966). One-man show of sculpture group, *Judgment of Paris* (together with newly completed plaster *Goddess with the Golden Thighs,* cast in bronze 1966), Egan Gallery (September). Included in "Roots of Abstract Art in America 1910-30," National Collection of Fine Arts, Smithsonian Institution, Washington, D.C. (December-January 1966). Begins two large plasters for bronzes, *Minerva* (final figure for *Judgment of Paris* group) and *Hiroshima*.

1966 Bronze cast of *Goddess with the Golden Thighs*. Completes *Hiroshima, Minerva,* and revised version of *Birth of Venus*.

BIBLIOGRAPHY
compiled by Elita Taylor

As this is the first book to appear on Nakian, every effort has been made to compile as complete a bibliography as possible, with the exception of short reviews and references in general works on sculpture. Most of the material cited can be found in the Library of The Museum of Modern Art and the New York Public Library. To parallel the account of events in the artist's career in the "Biographical Outline," pages 39-47, and indicate the growth of interest in his work, entries have been arranged chronologically within each category: Statements by the Artist (nos. 1-6); Articles and Critiques, including reviews of one-man shows (nos. 7-54); Catalogues: One-Man Shows (nos. 55-62), and Catalogues: Group Exhibitions (nos. 63-105). Reviews of group exhibitions, when cited, are listed with the respective catalogues.

STATEMENTS BY NAKIAN

1933 See bibl. 12.

1934 See bibl. 15.

1938 1. "European atmosphere" on island delights artist. *Staten Island Advance,* Dec. 6, 1938.
      Interview.

1952 See bibl. 22.

1954 2. (Statement.) 10 artists in the margin. Edited by Belle Krasne. *Design Quarterly,* no. 30, p. 14-15 ill., 1954.

1958 3. (Statement.) Is today's artist with or against the past? *Art News,* v. 57, no. 4, p. 29 ill., June 1958.
      Recorded by Thomas B. Hess; one of 12 interviews with American artists conducted by editors of *Art News.*

1960 4. Ego and eternity, a dialogue on Late Egyptian art. *Art News,* v. 59, no. 7, p. 28-30 ill., Nov. 1960.
      With Bernard V. Bothmer, Curator, Brooklyn Museum.
      See also bibl. 27 and 28.

1961 5. Dedication of exterior art. *The Villager* (New York), p. 4, 13 ill., July 20, 1961.
      Interview preceding dedication of Nakian's sculpture for façade of Loeb Student Center, New York University.
      See also bibl. 31.

1962 See bibl. 42.

1963 See bibl. 47.

1964 6. (Art, New York: Reuben Nakian, sculptor, interviewed by Thomas B. Hess.) New York, Nov. 4, 1964.
      TV broadcast on Channel 13, WNDT, produced by Colin Clark; repeated Nov. 6, 1964 and Feb. 4, 1965. Kinescope in possession of Junior Council of Museum of Modern Art.

1965 See bibl. 51.

ARTICLES AND CRITIQUES
includes reviews of one-man shows

1922 7. (Reproduction: *Jack Rabbit.*) *Dial,* v. 72, no. 5, p. 464 a, May 1922.
      Short biography on inside cover.

1926 8. W(atson), F(orbes. Nakian). *The Arts,* v. 10, no. 6, p. 345, 346-347 ill., Dec. 1926.
      Review of Nakian's first one-man show, Whitney Studio Club.

1930 9. Goodrich, Lloyd. November exhibitions: Julia Kelly and Reuben Nakian. *The Arts,* v. 17, no. 2, p. 121-122, Nov. 1930.
      Review of Downtown Gallery exhibition (bibl. 55).

      10. Breuning, Margaret. Watercolors, paintings, prints, sculpture, all on week's art calendar (Nakian). *New York Evening Post,* p. 7 ill., Nov. 1, 1930.
      Review of Downtown Gallery exhibition.

1933 11. Reuben Nakian's sculpture. *New York Sun,* p. 23 ill., Mar. 4, 1933.
      Review of Downtown Gallery exhibition (bibl. 56).

      12. Cross, Louise. Artists' portraits by Reuben Nakian, Downtown Gallery. *Creative Art,* v. 12, no. 4, p. 302-303 ill., Apr. 1933.
      Review of Downtown Gallery exhibition. Includes notes from conversation with artist.

1934 13. Pousette-Dart, Nathaniel. Reuben Nakian...

48

a master of form. *Studio News* (New York), v. 5, no. 2, p. 6, 7, 9 ill., Feb. 1934.

14. McB(ride), H(enry). Babe Ruth in sculpture. *New York Sun,* p. 11 ill., Feb. 17, 1934.
Review of Downtown Gallery exhibition.

15. Wedge, Will. A ton of clay to make Ruth. *New York Sun,* p. 31, Feb. 20, 1934.
Review of *Babe Ruth* at Downtown Gallery. Includes statements by artist (reprinted in part in *Art Digest,* v. 8, no. 11, p. 13, Mar. 1, 1934, and *Scholastic,* v. 24, no. 11, p. 26, Apr. 21, 1934).

1935 16. Jewell, Edward Alden. Busts of leaders at Capital shown. *New York Times,* p. 19, May 1, 1935.
Review of Downtown Gallery exhibition (bibl. 57).

17. Mumford, Lewis. Portraits in plaster. *New Yorker,* v. 11, no. 14, p. 69-70, May 18, 1935.
Review of Downtown Gallery exhibition.

18. (Reproductions: 6 plaster heads of Roosevelt cabinet members.) *Survey Graphic,* v. 24, no. 6, p. (296-297) ill., June 1935.
Selected from Downtown Gallery exhibition.

19. Reuben Nakian. *Index of twentieth century artists,* v. 2, no. 11, p. 165-166, Aug. 1935.
Includes bibliography and exhibitions list (1922-34).

1949 20. (de)K(ooning), E(laine). Reviews and previews: Reuben Nakian's. *Art News,* v. 48, no. 3, p. 42-43 ill., May 1949.
Review of Egan Gallery exhibition.

21. Preston, Stuart. Sculpture by Nakian. *New York Times,* Section II, p. 8, May 8, 1949.
Review of Egan Gallery exhibition.

1952 22. Voyage to Crete. *Time,* v. 59, no. 19, p. 80 ill., May 12, 1952.
Review of Egan Gallery exhibition. Includes statements by artist.

1958 23. Hess, Thomas B. Introducing the steel sculpture of Nakian: *The Rape of Lucrece. Art News,* v. 57, no. 7 (part 1), p. 36-39, 65-66 ill., cover, Nov. 1958.

24. Ashton, Dore. Art: Nakian's sculpture. *New York Times,* p. 30, Nov. 14, 1958.
Review of Stewart-Marean Gallery exhibition (bibl. 58).

1959 25. Hess, Thomas B. U.S. sculpture, some recent directions. *Portfolio & Art News Annual,* no. 1, p. 112-127, 146, 148, 150-152 ill., 1959.

26. Kramer, Hilton. Month in review (Nakian). *Arts,* v. 33, no. 4, p. 48-50 ill., Jan. 1959.
Review of Stewart-Marean Gallery exhibition (bibl. 58).

1960 27. N.Y.U. commissions Nakian sculpture. *New York Herald Tribune,* Section I, p. 16, July 31, 1960.
Includes statement by artist on façade sculpture for Loeb Student Center, New York University (reprinted in *Architectural Record,* v. 129, no. 3, p. 303, Mar. 1961).

28. The crazy thing to do. *Newsweek,* v. 56, no. 22, p. 104-105 ill., Nov. 21, 1960.
Review of Egan Gallery exhibition. Includes statements by artist.

29. Porter, Fairfield. Art (Nakian). *Nation,* v. 191, no. 22, p. 512, Dec. 24, 1960.
Review of Egan Gallery exhibition.

1961 30. Goldwater, Robert. Reuben Nakian. *Quadrum,* no. 11, p. 95-102 ill. (1961).

31. Hess, Thomas B. Today's artists: Nakian. *Portfolio & Art News Annual,* no. 4, p. 84-99, 168-172 ill., 1961.
Includes statement by artist.

32. G(enauer), E(mily). Birds grounded by a sculptor. *New York Herald Tribune,* Section 4, p. 6, July 16, 1961.
On façade sculpture for Loeb Student Center, New York University. Reprints Nakian's 1960 statement (bibl. 27).

33. Conant, Howard. New York University collection: Nakian. *Art Journal,* v. 21, no. 1, p. 1, 22, cover ill., Fall 1961.
On façade sculpture for Loeb Student Center.

34. Adlow, Dorothy. Our daring sculptors. *Christian Science Monitor,* p. 10 ill., Sept. 2, 1961.
On façade sculpture for Loeb Student Center.

35. Rosenberg, Harold. Art in orbit. *Art News,* v. 60, no. 6, p. 22-26, 54, 57 ill., Oct. 1961.
Review of VI Bienal, São Paulo (bibl. 59). Main reference to Nakian, p. 54, p. 22 ill. (Revised version in Rosenberg's *The Anxious Object,* New York, Horizon, c. 1964.)

1962 36. O'Doherty, Brian. Art: mythmaking in the

20th century. *New York Times,* p. 34, March 20, 1962.
Review of Egan Gallery exhibition (bibl. 60).

37. Kozloff, Max. New York letter: Nakian. *Art International,* v. 6, no. 4, p. 82 ill., May 1962.
Review of Egan Gallery exhibition.

38. Seldis, Henry J. Show complements Nakian exuberance. *Los Angeles Times,* p. 12 ill., May 27, 1962.
Review of Los Angeles County Museum exhibition (bibl. 61).

39. Nordland, Gerald. An important Los Angeles showing. *Frontier* (Los Angeles), v. 13, no. 8, p. 21-23 ill., June 1962.
Review of Los Angeles County Museum exhibition.

40. S(ecunda), A(rthur). Reviews: Los Angeles: Reuben Nakian. *Artforum,* v. 1, no. 3, p. 4, 5 ill., Aug. 1962.
Review of Los Angeles County Museum exhibition.

41. Nordland, Gerald. Los Angeles letter: Southern California museums, *Kunstwerk,* v. 16, no. 4, p. 28, 35 ill., Oct. 1962.
Regarding Nakian acquisitions.

42. Gustaitis, Rasa. New Deal's busy sculptor back in town. *Washington Post,* p. B 3, Dec. 30, 1962.
Preceding Washington Gallery of Modern Art exhibition (bibl. 62). Includes statements by artist.

1963
43. Nakian in the capital. *Art News,* v. 61, no. 9, p. 25, 56 ill., Jan. 1963.
On Washington Gallery of Modern Art exhibition (bibl. 62).

44. Getlein, Frank. Art and artists: Reuben Nakian show at Gallery of Modern Art highly significant. *Sunday Star* (Washington), p. C 13, Jan 13, 1963.
Review of Washington Gallery of Modern Art exhibition.

45. Ahlander, Leslie Judd. Art in Washington: two events of major importance. *Washington Post,* p. G 8, Jan. 13, 1963.
Review of Washington Gallery of Modern Art exhibition.

46. (Reproductions and illustrations.) Reuben Na-
kian: studio, drawings, sculpture. *Location* (New York), no. 1, p. 8-15, Spring 1963.

47. Arnason, H(jorvardur) H(arvard). Nakian. *Art International,* v. 7, no. 4, p. 36-43 ill., April 1963.
Includes statements by artist.

1964
48. Hess, Thomas B. L'Après-midi d'un faune: drawings by Reuben Nakian. *Location* (New York), v. 1, no. 2, p. 43-54 ill., Summer 1964.
Includes 11 full-page illustrations.

49. Hess, Thomas B. November contrasts: Reuben Nakian. *Art News,* v. 63, no. 7, p. 30, 65 ill., Nov. 1964.
Review of Egan Gallery exhibition.

1965
50. Ashton, Dore. Visual pleasure from austerity (Nakian). *Studio International,* v. 169, no. 862, p. 94-95, Feb. 1965.
Review of Egan Gallery exhibition, Nov. 1964.

51. Kuh, Katharine. Portraits in paganism. *Saturday Review,* v. 48, no. 31, p. 28-29 ill., July 31, 1965.
Review of Egan Gallery exhibition, Summer. Includes statements by artist.

52. Lippard, Lucy R. New York letter (Nakian). *Art International,* v. 9, no. 8, p. 39, 42 ill., Nov. 1965.
Review of Egan Gallery exhibition, Sept.-Oct.

53. H(oene), A(nne). In the galleries: Reuben Nakian. *Arts,* v. 40, no. 1, p. 57-58 ill., Nov. 1965.
Review of Egan Gallery exhibition, Sept.-Oct.

1966
54. Hunter, Sam. American art since 1945. In *New Art Around the World,* edited by Sam Hunter (New York, Abrams, 1966—forthcoming).
Considerably revised and updated version of *Art since 1945,* New York, Abrams (1958).

CATALOGUES: ONE-MAN SHOWS

1930
55. New York. Downtown Gallery. Reuben Nakian. Oct. 28-Nov. 16, 1930.
Broadside. 7 works.

1933
56. New York. Downtown Gallery. Reuben Nakian: portraits of 10 artists. Feb. 27-Mar. 18, 1933. 2 p. ill. 10 works.

1935
57. Washington. Corcoran Gallery of Art. Portrait heads of officials of the present administration by Nakian. April 13-28, 1935.

4 p. Foreword by Henry McBride. 10 works. Exhibition also shown at Downtown Gallery, New York, May 1-18, 1935.

1958 58. New York. Stewart-Marean Gallery. Nakian. Nov. 12-Dec. 31, 1958.
    2 p. ill. 3 works. Exhibition selected and arranged by Charles Egan.

1961 59. São Paulo. Museu de Arte Moderna. VI Bienal. Estados Unidos (Nakian). Sept. 10-Dec. 31, 1961.
    40 p. ill. 48 works. Organized by The Museum of Modern Art. Nakian references, including text by Thomas B. Hess, p. 12-17 ill.; checklist p. 35-36.

1962 60. New York. Egan Gallery. Reuben Nakian. Mar. 19-Apr. 21, 1962.
    2 p. ill. 4 works.
    61. Los Angeles. County Museum of Art. Reuben Nakian, sculpture and drawings. May 16-June 26, 1962.
    8 p. ill. 52 works. Exhibition organized for VI Bienal, São Paulo (bibl. 59), including 6 works shown at Los Angeles only. Text by Robert Goldwater (reprinted from bibl. 30).

1963 62. Washington. Gallery of Modern Art. Nakian. Jan. 8-Feb. 18, 1963.
    17 p. ill. 13 sculptures; terra-cottas and drawings. Text by Thomas B. Hess.

CATALOGUES: GROUP EXHIBITIONS

1922 63. New York. Salons of America. Autumn Salon. Oct. 16-Nov. 4, 1922.
    p. (49). 1 work. Held at Anderson Galleries.

1923 64. New York. Whitney Studio Club. Exhibition of paintings by John Dos Passos and Adelaide J. Lawson and sculpture by Reuben Nakian. Jan. 5-24, 1923.
    p. (2-3). 6 works.
    65. New York. Salons of America. Spring Salon. May 21-June 9, 1923.
    p. (14). 1 work. Organized in cooperation with American Museum of Natural History and Brooklyn Institute of Arts and Sciences. Held at galleries of American Art Association.
    Reviewed in *The Arts* (New York), v. 3, no. 6, p. 427-428, June 1923.

1924 66. Chicago. Art Institute. 37th annual exhibition of American paintings and sculpture. Oct. 30-Dec. 14, 1924.
    p. (44, 61) ill. 1 work. (Nakian listed as "Vakian.")

1926 67. New York. Wildenstein Galleries. The exhibition of tri-national art: French, British, American. Jan. 26-Feb. 17, 1926.
    p. (14). 1 work.

1929 68. Chicago. Art Institute. 42nd annual exhibition of American paintings and sculpture. Oct. 24-Dec. 8, 1929.
    p. (60, 61) ill. 1 work.

1930 69. New York. Downtown Gallery. 33 moderns …paintings, sculpture, watercolors, drawings & prints by 33 American contemporary artists. Jan. 28-Feb. 15, 1930.
    p. (8-9, 23) ill. 6 works. Held at Grand Central Galleries.
    Reviewed by William McCormick in *New York American*, p. E 11, Feb. 2, 1930.

1932 70. New York. Whitney Museum of American Art. Exhibition of the American Society of Painters, Sculptors & Gravers. Feb. 6-28, 1932.
    p. (12). 2 works.

1933 71. New York. Whitney Museum of American Art. Exhibition of the work of artist fellows of the John Simon Guggenheim Memorial Foundation. April 3-27, 1933.
    p. (20, 27). 2 works.
    72. Chicago. Art Institute. Century of progress exhibition of paintings and sculpture: lent from American collections. June 1-Nov. 1, 1933.
    p. 111. 1 work.
    73. New York. Whitney Museum of American Art. First biennial exhibition of contemporary American sculpture, watercolors and prints. Dec. 5, 1933-Jan. 11, 1934.
    p. 7, 29. 1 work.

1934 74. Philadelphia. Pennsylvania Academy of the Fine Arts. 129th annual exhibition. Jan. 28-Feb. 25, 1934.
    p. 49, 61. 1 work.
    75. New York. First municipal art exhibition: paintings, sculpture, drawings, prints by living American artists identified with the New York art world. Feb. 28-March 31, 1934.

p. 21. 2 works. Held at The Forum, RCA Building, Rockefeller Center. Sponsored by the Hon. Fiorello La Guardia, Mayor of the City of New York.

76. New York. Museum of Modern Art. Modern works of art: fifth anniversary exhibition. Nov. 20, 1934-Jan. 20, 1935.

    p. 37, (144) ill. 1 work. Text by Alfred H. Barr, Jr.

77. New York. Downtown Gallery. Practical manifestations in American art. Dec. 13-31, 1934.

    2 p. 2 works.

1935 78. Newark. Museum. George Overbury "Pop" Hart. Oct. 10-Dec. 5, 1935.

    p. 61. 2 works.

79. Chicago. Art Institute. 46th annual exhibition of American paintings and sculpture. Oct. 24-Dec. 8, 1935.

    p. (21). 1 work.

1936 80. Buffalo. Fine Arts Academy, Albright Art Gallery. The art of today. Jan. 3-31, 1936.

    p. 13. 3 works.

81. New York. Whitney Museum of American Art. Second biennial exhibition, part one: sculpture, drawings, and prints. Jan. 14-Feb. 13, 1936.

    p. (6). 1 work.

1938 82. Paris. Musée du Jeu de Paume. Trois siècles d'art aux Etats-Unis. May-July 1938.

    p. 33, 50. 1 work. Organized by Museum of Modern Art, New York. Text, "Painting and Sculpture in the U.S.," by Alfred H. Barr, Jr.

83. Washington. Museum of Modern Art Gallery. Modern American and European sculpture. Dec. 11, 1938-Jan. 22, 1939.

    p. (3). 1 work.

1939 84. New York. Museum of Modern Art. Art in our time. May 10-Sept. 30, 1939.

    p. 250 ill. 1 work.

85. New York. Whitney Museum of American Art. Twentieth century artists: a selection from the Museum's permanent collection. Sept. 13-Dec. 3, 1939.

    p. (14). 1 work.

86. Chicago. Art Institute. Half a century of American art. Nov. 16, 1939-Jan. 7, 1940.

    p. 59. 1 work.

1944 87. New York. Durand-Ruel Galleries. Kelekian as the artist sees him. Oct. 17-Nov. 4, 1944.

    p. (4, 19) ill. 1 work. Foreword by Frank Crowninshield.

88. Newark. Museum. A museum in action:... American paintings and sculpture from the Museum's collections....Oct. 31, 1944-Jan. 31, 1945.

    p. 60, 166, 182. 1 work. Introduction by Holger Cahill.

1947 89. New York. Federation of Modern Painters and Sculptors. Seventh annual exhibition of paintings and sculpture by guests of members....Sept. 9-27, 1947.

    p. (4). 1 work. Exhibition held at Wildenstein & Co.

    Reviewed in *Art Digest,* v. 21, no. 20, p. 10, Sept. 15, 1947.

1949 90. New York. Whitney Museum of American Art. Annual exhibition of contemporary American sculpture, watercolors, and drawings. Apr. 2-May 8, 1949.

    p. (9). 1 work.

1959 91. New York. Museum of Modern Art. Recent Sculpture, U.S.A. May 13-Aug. 16, 1959.

    p. (24, 39) ill. 2 works. Sponsored by the Junior Council of the Museum; subsequently circulated to 4 cities in the U.S. Catalogue published as *Bulletin,* v. 26, no. 3, Spring 1959.

1961 92. Chicago. Art Institute. 64th American exhibition: paintings, sculpture. Jan. 6-Feb. 5, 1961.

    p. (31). 1 work.

93. New York. Great Jones Gallery. Heads by eight sculptors. Sept. 19-Oct. 15, 1961.

    p. (3). 1 work.

    Reviewed by Sidney Tillim in *Arts,* v. 36, no. 1, p. 36-38, Oct. 1961.

1962 94. Hartford. Wadsworth Atheneum. Continuity and change: 45 American abstract painters and sculptors. Apr. 12-May 27, 1962.

    p. 4, 31 ill. 6 works. Foreword by Samuel Wagstaff, Jr.

    Reviewed by Dorothy Adlow in *Christian Science Monitor,* p. 12 ill., May 4, 1962.

95. Newark. Museum. A survey of American sculpture: late 18th century to 1962. May 10-Oct. 20, 1962.

    p. 26, 35. 2 works. Text by William H. Gerdts.

96. New York. Solomon R. Guggenheim Mu-

seum. Modern sculpture from the Joseph H. Hirshhorn collection. Oct. 3, 1962-Jan. 6, 1963.

    p. 160, 174, 224-225, 241 ill. 8 works. Commentary by H. H. Arnason.

1963 97. Chicago. Art Institute. 66th annual American exhibition. Jan. 11-Feb. 10, 1963.

    p. (8, 29) ill. 1 work.

98. London. County Council. Sculpture: open-air exhibition of contemporary British and American works. May-Sept. 1963.

    p. (17-18, 23, 53) ill. 1 work. U.S. section organized by Museum of Modern Art, New York. Held at Battersea Park.

99. Washington. Gallery of Modern Art. Sculptors of our time. Sept. 17-Oct. 31, 1963.

    p. (22, 16) ill. 1 work.

1964 100. New York. Solomon R. Guggenheim Museum. American drawings. Sept. 17-Oct. 28, 1964.

    p. (35, 55, 63) ill. 4 works. Introduction by Lawrence Alloway. Includes bibliography of artist.

101. New York. New School Art Center. The artist's reality: an international sculpture exhibition. Oct. 14-Nov. 14, 1964.

    p. (20) ill. 1 work.

1965 102. Providence. Art Club. Critics' choice: Art since World War II. March 31-Apr. 24, 1965.

    p. 13, 16, 36 ill. 1 work. 6th Kane Memorial Exhibition, sponsored by Providence Art Club, Museum of Rhode Island School of Design and Brown University.

103. Mexico, D. F. Universidad Nacional Autónoma de Mexico. Actitudes plásticas. June-July 1965.

    p. 15-17 ill. 3 works. Introduction by Harold Rosenberg.

104. Paris. Musée Rodin. Etats-Unis: Sculptures du XXe siècle. June 22-Oct. 15, 1965.

    p. 46-47 ill. 5 works. Organized by Museum of Modern Art, New York. Subsequently shown at Berlin, Hochschule für Bildende Künste, Nov. 20, 1965-Jan 9, 1966, and Baden-Baden, Staatliche Kunsthalle, Mar.-Apr. 1966.

105. Washington. National Collection of Fine Arts, Smithsonian Institution. Roots of abstract art in America 1910-1930. Dec. 2, 1965-Jan. 9, 1966.

    p. 30, (87). 1 work.

CATALOGUE
OF THE EXHIBITION
June 20—September 5, 1966

The following catalogue is divided into two sections, sculpture and drawings, each arranged chronologically. Nakian does not inscribe his works with dates; but he, his assistant Larry McCabe, and his dealer Charles Egan have kindly provided information as to years of execution, according to the best available records and their own recollection.

For sculpture, the greatest dimension is given; for drawings, height precedes width. An asterisk indicates that the work is illustrated.

SCULPTURE

*1. *Head of Marcel Duchamp.* 1943. Bronze, 21¾" high. The Joseph H. Hirshhorn Collection. Ill. p. 12.

*2. *Europa and the Bull.* 1945. Bronze, 10½" high. Private collection. Ill. p. 20.

3. *Shepherd with a Lyre.* 1946. Terra-cotta, 9½" high. Collection Mr. and Mrs. Thor Bostrom.

*4. *Ecstasy.* 1946-47. Bronze (cast 1961), 12½" high. The Joseph H. Hirshhorn Collection. Ill. p. 12.

*5. *Europa Series.* 1948. Terra-cotta, 12¾" high. Egan Gallery. Ill. p. 20.

*6. *Pastorale.* 1948. Terra-cotta, 15⅝" high. Collection Donald Droll. Ill. p. 20 and back cover.

*7. *Salome.* 1948. Terra-cotta with gold leaf, 6" high. Collection Mr. and Mrs. Philip M. Stern. Ill. p. 12.

*8. *Europa.* 1949. Terra-cotta, 15" high. Collection Mr. and Mrs. Thor Bostrom. Ill. p. 22.

*9. *Voyage to Crete.* 1949. Terra-cotta, 26" long. Collection Mr. and Mrs. Thomas B. Hess. Ill. p. 26.

*10. *Europa and the Bull.* 1949-50. Terra-cotta, 27" high. The Joseph H. Hirshhorn Collection. Ill. p. 13.

*11. *Europa and the Bull.* 1950. Terra-cotta, painted, 9½" high. Egan Gallery. Ill. p. 13.

12. *Europa Series.* 1950. Terra-cotta, 18" high. Collection Mr. and Mrs. Lee V. Eastman.

*13. *Paris.* 1950. Bronze (cast 1961), 9¼" high. Private collection. Ill. p. 20.

*14. *Heraldic Figures.* c. 1950-54. Terra-cotta, 8¼"
high. Collection Mr. and Mrs. Thomas B. Hess.
Ill. p. 26.

*15. *Herodias.* 1952. Bronze (cast 1961), 44" high. Estate of Mrs. Henry Epstein. Ill. p. 18.

*16. *Study for Voyage to Crete.* 1952. Terra-cotta, 8"
high. Collection Mr. and Mrs. Thomas B. Hess.
Ill. p. 26.

*17. *Voyage to Crete.* 1952. Terra-cotta, 28" high. Collection Margot Stewart. Ill. p. 13.

*18. *La Chambre à Coucher de l'Empereur.* 1954.
Bronze (cast 1958), 70" long. Collection Mr. and
Mrs. Philip M. Stern. Ill. p. 10.

19. *Odalisque, Number 1 (Study for the Rape of Lucrece).* 1954. Terra-cotta, 8" long. Egan Gallery.

20. *Odalisque, Number 2 (Study for The Rape of Lucrece).* 1954. Terra-cotta, 7¾" long. Egan Gallery.

21. *Odalisque, Number 3 (Study for The Rape of Lucrece).* 1954. Terra-cotta, 9" long. Egan Gallery.

22. *Odalisque, Number 4 (Study for The Rape of Lucrece).* 1954. Terra-cotta, 9½" long. Egan Gallery.

*23. *The Rape of Lucrece.* 1955-58. Welded steel,
painted, 12'11" long. The Museum of Modern
Art (extended loan from Egan Gallery). Ill. p. 17.

24. *Europa and the Bull.* 1956. Terra-cotta, 10" long.
Egan Gallery.

*25. *The Burning Walls of Troy.* 1957. Terra-cotta,
11½" long. Egan Gallery. Ill. p. 19.

26. *Chamber Piece.* 1957. Terra-cotta, 12½" long.
Egan Gallery.

27. *Europa and the Bull.* 1957-58. Terra-cotta, 13¼"
long. Egan Gallery.

28. *Europa and the Bull.* 1957-58. Terra-cotta, 11"
long. Egan Gallery.

29. *Europa Series.* 1958. Terra-cotta, 14" long. Egan
Gallery.

30. *Europa Series.* 1958. Terra-cotta, 11" high. Egan
Gallery.

*31. *Rape of Lucrece Series.* 1958. Terra-cotta, 16"
long. The Museum of Modern Art (gift of the
artist in memory of Holger Cahill). Ill. p. 27.

*32. *Rock Drawing.* 1958. Terra-cotta, 16" long. The
Museum of Modern Art (fund given in memory
of Philip L. Goodwin). Ill. p. 27.

33. *Venus and Adonis.* 1958. Terra-cotta, 12¼" long.
Egan Gallery.

*34. *Europa and the Bull.* 1958-60. Terra-cotta, 17"
long. Collection Mrs. Robert M. Benjamin. Ill.
p. 29.

*35. *The Duchess of Alba.* 1959. Welded steel, painted, 10' long. Los Angeles County Museum of Art.
Ill. p. 15.

36. *Duchess of Alba Series.* 1959. Terra-cotta, 12¼"
long. Egan Gallery.

37. *Europa and the Bull.* 1959. Terra-cotta, 10½"
long. Egan Gallery.

38. *Stone Drawing (Europa).* 1959. Terra-cotta, 9¼"
long. Egan Gallery.

39. *Abstraction.* 1959-60. Terra-cotta, 13½" long.
Egan Gallery.

*40. *Duchess of Alba Series.* 1959-60. Terra-cotta,
14¼" long. Los Angeles County Museum of Art
(Museum Associates Purchase; Contemporary Art
Council Fund). Ill. p. 14.

41. *Europa Series.* 1959-60. Bronze (cast 1961), 18"
long. Collection Mr. and Mrs. Lee V. Eastman.

42. *Europa Series.* 1959-60. Terra-cotta, 12" long.
Collection Mr. and Mrs. Robert B. Eichholz.

43. *Europa Series.* 1959-60. Terra-cotta, 15½" long.
Egan Gallery.

*44. *Europa Series.* 1959-60. Terra-cotta, 12½" long.
Egan Gallery. Ill. p. 22.

45. *Europa Series.* 1959-60. Terra-cotta, 13¼" long.
Egan Gallery.

46. *Leda and the Swan.* 1959-60. Bronze, 22" long.
Donald Morris Gallery.

*47. *Mars and Venus.* 1959-60. Welded steel, painted,
13' long. Egan Gallery. Ill. p. 25.

*48. *Mars and Venus Series.* 1959-60. Terra-cotta, 15"
long. Egan Gallery. Ill. p. 25.

49. *Europa.* 1960. Bronze (cast 1961), 18" long. The
Joseph H. Hirshhorn Collection.

*50. *Europa Series.* 1960. Terra-cotta, 8" high. Egan
Gallery. Ill. p. 29.

51. *Europa Series.* 1960. Bronze (cast 1961), 18½"
long. Egan Gallery.

*52. *Leda and the Swan.* 1960. Bronze (cast 1961),
6½" high. Collection Mr. and Mrs. Warren
Brandt. Ill. p. 30.

*53. *Nymph and Centaur.* 1960. Terra-cotta, 15" long.
Egan Gallery. Ill. p. 21.

*54. *Salome and Herodias with the Head of John the Baptist.* 1960. Terra-cotta: *Salome,* 10″ long; *Herodias,* 9¼″ long; *Head of John the Baptist,* 4″ high. Collection Mr. and Mrs. Thomas B. Hess. Ill. p. 31.

*55. *Voyage to Crete.* 1960. Bronze, 41″ high. Collection Mr. and Mrs. Philip M. Stern. Ill. p. 18.

*56. *Voyage to Crete.* 1960. Bronze, 33″ high. Egan Gallery. Ill. p. 18.

57. *Europa Series.* 1960-61. Terra-cotta, 16½″ long. Egan Gallery.

58. *Leda and the Swan Series.* 1960-61. Bronze (cast 1963), 6¾″ high. Egan Gallery.

*59. *Europa Series.* 1960-62. Terra-cotta, 11″ long. Egan Gallery. Ill. p. 31.

*60. *Hecuba.* 1960-62. Bronze (cast 1963), 7′ high. Collection Mr. and Mrs. George S. Rosenthal. Ill. p. 34.

*61. *Olympia.* 1960-62. Bronze (cast 1963), 6′ high. Whitney Museum of American Art (gift of the Friends of the Whitney Museum). Ill. p. 33.

*62. *Trojan Woman.* 1960-62. Plaster and steel, 9′ 1″ high. Egan Gallery. Ill. p. 32.

63. *Abstraction.* 1961. Terra-cotta, 14″ long. Los Angeles County Museum of Art.

64. *Abstraction.* 1961. Terra-cotta, 13½″ long. Egan Gallery.

65. *Europa and the Bull.* 1961. Terra-cotta, 12″ long. Egan Gallery.

66. *Europa and the Bull.* 1962. Bronze (cast 1963), 10½″ long. Collection Mr. and Mrs. George S. Heyer, Jr.

*67. *Europa Series.* 1962. Bronze, 11″ high. Collection Mr. and Mrs. J. Lee Johnson III. Ill. p. 30.

68. *Europa Series.* 1962. Terra-cotta, 8″ high. Egan Gallery.

69. *Leda and the Swan.* 1962. Terra-cotta, 11″ high. Collection Emile Dubrule.

*70. *Leda and the Swan.* 1962. Terra-cotta, 14¼″ long. (Inscribed on reverse "To Marilyn"; completed on hearing of Marilyn Monroe's death, August 4, 1962.) Collection Mr. and Mrs. Thomas B. Hess. Ill. p. 21.

71. *Leda and the Swan.* 1962. Terra-cotta, 15½″ long. Collection Mrs. Bliss Parkinson.

72. *Leda and the Swan.* 1962. Terra-cotta, 15½″ long. Egan Gallery.

*73. *Leda and the Swan.* 1962. Terra-cotta, 12″ long. Egan Gallery. Ill. p. 28.

74. *Leda and the Swan.* 1962. Terra-cotta, 14″ long. Egan Gallery.

75. *Leda and the Swan.* 1962. Bronze (cast 1963), 8½″ high. Egan Gallery.

76. *Nymph and Goat.* 1962. Terra-cotta, 16″ high. Collection Mr. and Mrs. Philip M. Stern.

77. *Study for Paris.* 1962. Terra-cotta, 13½″ high. Egan Gallery.

78. *Study for Venus.* 1962. Terra-cotta, 11¼″ high. Egan Gallery.

79. *Study for Venus.* 1962. Terra-cotta, 13½″ high. Egan Gallery.

80. *Europa Series.* 1963. Bronze, 6½″ high. Collection David P. Bassine.

81. *Europa Series.* 1963. Bronze, 9½″ long. Egan Gallery.

82. *Juno.* 1963. Terra-cotta, 8½″ long. Egan Gallery.

*83. *Leda and the Swan.* 1963. Bronze, 9½″ long. Collection Mrs. Eleanor Berkson. Ill. p. 28.

*84. *Leda and the Swan.* 1963. Bronze, 12½″ long. Egan Gallery. Ill. p. 28.

85. *Leda and the Swan.* 1963. Bronze, 9″ long. Egan Gallery.

86. *Leda and the Swan.* 1963. Bronze, 9½″ high. Egan Gallery.

87. *Leda and the Swan.* 1963. Bronze, 6″ high. Egan Gallery.

88. *Minerva.* 1963. Terra-cotta, 8½″ long. Egan Gallery.

89. *Paris.* 1963. Terra-cotta, 10½″ long. Egan Gallery.

90. *Venus.* 1963. Terra-cotta, 10¼″ long. Egan Gallery.

*91. *Judgment of Paris: Paris.* 1963-64. Plaster, 6′ 6½″ high. Egan Gallery. Ill. p. 36.

*92. *Birth of Venus.* 1963-66. Plaster, 10′ 11″ long. Egan Gallery. Ill. p. 35 and front cover.

93. *Nymph and Satyr.* 1964. Bronze, 8″ high. Collection David P. Bassine.

*94. *Goddess with the Golden Thighs.* 1964-65. Bronze (cast 1966), 12′6″ long. Egan Gallery. Ill. p. 6.

*95. *Judgment of Paris: Juno.* 1964-65. Plaster, 6′ 11″ high. Egan Gallery. Ill. p. 37.

*96. *Judgment of Paris: Venus.* 1964-65. Plaster, 7' 4" long. Egan Gallery. Ill. p. 37.

97. *Nymph and Satyr Series.* 1964-65. Terra-cotta, 12" long. Collection Charles Brickbauer.

98. *Nymph and Satyr Series.* 1964-65. Terra-cotta, 15" high. Collection Mr. and Mrs. Alvin S. Lane.

99. *Europa and the Bull.* 1965. Bronze (cast 1966), 24" high. Egan Gallery.

100-103. *Relief I, Relief II, Relief III, Relief IV.* 1965. Bronze, each 28" long. Egan Gallery.

*104. *Hiroshima.* 1965-66. Plaster, 9' high. Egan Gallery. Ill. p. 46.

*105. *Judgment of Paris: Minerva.* 1965-66. Plaster, 8' 1" high. Egan Gallery. Ill. p. 37.

DRAWINGS

106. *Odalisque.* 1954. Sepia on paper, 12¾ x 17¾". Egan Gallery.

107. *Odalisque.* 1954. Sepia on paper, 12⅞ x 19¾". Egan Gallery.

108. *Odalisque.* 1954. Ink on paper, 11 x 13½". Egan Gallery.

109. *Odalisque.* 1954. Ink on paper, 14 x 16½". Egan Gallery.

110. *Herodias with the Head of John the Baptist.* 1958. Ink on paper, 16½ x 14". Egan Gallery.

*111-113. *Duchess of Alba Series.* 1959-60. Ink wash on paper, respectively 8½ x 11", 8½ x 11", and 12¼ x 14¼". Los Angeles County Museum of Art (Museum Associates Purchase; Contemporary Art Council Fund). Ill. p. 14.

*114. *Europa.* 1959-60. Ink on paper, 14⅛ x 16¾". Egan Gallery. Ill. p. 23.

115. *Europa.* 1959-60. Ink on paper, 14 x 17". Egan Gallery.

*116. *Europa.* 1959-60. Ink on paper, 14 x 16⅝". Egan Gallery. Ill. p. 23.

117. *Europa.* 1959-60. Ink on paper, 13⅞ x 16⅝". Egan Gallery.

*118. *Europa.* 1959-60. Ink on paper, 14 x 16⅝". Egan Gallery. Ill. p. 23.

*119. *Europa.* 1959-60. Ink on paper, 14⅛ x 16⅝". Egan Gallery. Ill. p. 23.

*120. *Europa Series.* 1959-60. Brush and ink, 14 x 16¾". The Museum of Modern Art (extended loan from Egan Gallery). Ill. p. 24.

*121. *Mars and Venus Series.* 1959-60. Wash, brush and ink, 14 x 16⅞". The Museum of Modern Art (gift of Charles Egan in memory of J. B. Neumann). Ill. p. 24.

*122. *Mars and Venus Series.* 1959-60. Wash, brush and ink, 11¾ x 17⅝". Egan Gallery. Ill. p. 25.

123. *Mars and Venus Series.* 1959-60. Ink on paper, 14 x 17". Egan Gallery.

124. *Mars and Venus Series.* 1959-60. Ink on paper, 11¾ x 17⅜". Egan Gallery.

*125. *Hecuba Series.* 1960-62. Wash, brush and ink, 16⅝ x 14". The Museum of Modern Art (extended loan from Egan Gallery). Ill. p. 24.

126. *Europa.* 1961. Ink on paper, 14 x 16½". Egan Gallery.

127. *Leda.* 1962-63. Ink on paper, 14 x 16¾". Egan Gallery.

128. *Leda and the Swan.* 1962-63. Ink on paper, 14 x 16¾". Egan Gallery.

129. *Leda and the Swan.* 1962-63. Ink on paper, 14 x 16½". Egan Gallery.

130. *Leda and the Swan.* 1962-63. Ink on paper, 13⅛ x 16½". Egan Gallery.

131. *Leda.* 1964. Ink on paper, 14 x 16½". Egan Gallery.

132. *Nymph and Goat.* 1964. Ink on paper, 14 x 16¾". Egan Gallery.

133. *Nymph and Goat.* 1964. Ink on paper, 17¾ x 12". Egan Gallery.

134. *Judgment of Paris Series: Juno.* 1966. Ink and brush on paper, 17¾ x 12". Egan Gallery.

135. *Judgment of Paris Series: Minerva.* 1966. Ink and brush on paper. 17¾ x 12". Egan Gallery.

136. *Judgment of Paris Series: Venus.* 1966. Ink and brush on paper. 17¾ x 12". Egan Gallery.

137. *Judgment of Paris Series: Venus.* 1966. Ink and brush on paper. 17¾ x 12". Egan Gallery.

138. *Venus and Adonis.* 1966. Ink on paper, 16¾ x 14". Egan Gallery.

139. *Venus and Adonis.* 1966. Ink on paper, 16⅝ x 14". Egan Gallery.